Conflict Healing

Relational Health

■ ■ ■

By Prince Handley

University of Excellence Press

Copyright © 2012 by Prince Handley
All Rights Reserved.

UNIVERSITY OF EXCELLENCE PRESS
Los Angeles ■ London ■ Tel Aviv

ISBN-13: 978-0692345344
ISBN-10: 0692345345

First Edition

The conflict resolution book you need

TABLE OF CONTENTS

FOREWORD

The content of this book is developed in two sections:

    How to Deal with Tension in Relationships

    How to Resolve Conflicts the Bible Way.

The first section deals with **different "mentalities"** and how to strengthen your relationships—and your human psyche—while dealing with tension.

The second section deals with different trespasses and offenses—**categories of problems**—that must be addressed if we are to progress in our mental and emotional (and sometimes physical) growth ... and, especially, in our spiritual growth with the LORD.

Both sections of the book include **"How To Do It" guidelines** that work, PLUS examples—**real life and personal examples**—some, even embarrassing.

The reason the book is presented in these two formats is first, to help the reader recognize the **different personality dynamics involved and the processes for resolving pertinent issues**—and, secondly, to

discover exact Biblical principles for successful conflict resolution. It works! Give it a try, and spend the rest of your life in peace, power and production!

Conflict Healing

Relational Health

■ ■ ■

HOW TO DEAL WITH TENSION IN RELATIONSHIPS

Tension in relationships is NOT bad. It is a "way mark" if handled correctly. That is, it is a marker along the way to further progress, an ensign for the strengthening of the relationship.

There are four (4) types of mentalities:

- Survival

- Contract

- Traditional (family)

- Covenant

In the covenant relationship, you are being concerned **MORE for the other party**. Dr. Livingstone, the great missionary to Africa, reached many tribes for Christ that could not have been reached otherwise by making a blood covenant with them.

In such covenant relationships each party is telling the other: "Whatever I have is yours if you need it." Livingstone had a life threatening condition that required him to drink goats' milk. Because of this, he would keep a goat with him. One day, a tribal chieftain that had made a blood covenant with Livingstone told him that **he wanted his white goat**. That reminds me of the saying "Got your goat!" Knowing the seriousness of this request, and the danger it could pose for himself, Livingstone honored the request and gave the chieftain his white goat.

Many of our problems appear in our relationships with other people. Has anyone ever had problems with you?

Moses was a problem solver; he was an intercessor. You can read about his intercession and leadership through using prayer in Numbers Chapter 14. The FIRST thing to do when tension arises in a relationship is to PRAY.

Because there are problems in interpersonal relationships does NOT mean you are sinning; for example, problems with family members. If you are praying for the other person or people, if you are forgiving, and if you are doing what the Holy Spirit is showing you to do (which never contradicts scripture), then be at peace. However, many people—**and some Christians**—"stumble" in life because they are proceeding in darkness. Some Christians even experience lots of sickness and repeated physical conditions—or even accidents—because of this.

Our beloved brother John admonishes us in his writings as follows:

"He who says he is in the light, and hates his brother, is in darkness until now.

He who loves his brother abides in the light, and there is no cause for stumbling in him.

But he who hates his brother is in darkness and walks in darkness, and does not know where he is going, because the darkness has blinded his eyes." (1 John 2:9-11)

This is also why it is important NOT to cause trouble in a relationship between other people. The Bible says that one of the seven things that are an abomination to God, and that he hates, is the person *"who causes discord among brethren."* (Proverbs 6:19)

CAUTION

If a person who is NOT in either a traditional (family blood) relationship with you or a covenant relationship with you, **comes to you and says something negatively about**, or brings charges against, **a person in your family or with whom you are in relationship**, **BEWARE!** Many families and relationships have been injured by such people. Your first reaction / response should be as follows: *"I will consult with my relative or partner about this (what you have told me) and then I will pray and take it to the Lord."*

Many people have received lies about their own family members or partners while never having even asked about "the other side of the story," or WHY the accusations have been made, or even IF they were true. My mother used to say, "Blood is thicker than water."

Moses led 3,000,000 people. In Numbers Chapter 14, Moses had just finished asking—interceding—for God's mercy on Israel when Korah, Dathan, and Abiram started their rebellion against him. Korah was Moses' cousin and a member of the tribe of Levi in the family of Aaron. (Numbers 16:3)

Notice five (5) processes in the life of Moses in dealing with tension in relationships and solving problems:

- Personal Prayer

- Confrontation

- Let God Fight for You

- Separate Yourself from Strife

10

PERSONAL PRAYER

In Numbers 16:4-7 notice that Moses positioned himself face down in prayer. First, always PRAY and SEEK GOD'S WISDOM. Are you facing a problem? Are you causing a problem?

Korah's complaint against Aaron was strictly a complaint against God: it was not a complaint about qualifications, but against God's order. This can often be a cause of spiritual impotence . . . and of judgment . . . among churches, ministries, or families.

In 1 Corinthians 11: 3 we see God's order for the home:

"But I want you to know that the head of every man is Christ, the head of the woman is man, and the head of Christ is God."

It is NOT a matter of who is better than another, **but rather of order, so that love and power can flow** unhindered from God: to effect BLESSING upon the unit and upon the individuals of the unit. In cases where an individual is NOT performing their duties ...

for example, **when a man is not being the spiritual leader of the home, then God has ways to circumvent the hindrance so that blessing will flow.** This is where prayer and obedience come into play by each member. PRAY, LISTEN, and OBEY!

CONFRONTATION

Dathan and Abiram were members of the tribe of Reuben, while Moses was of the tribe of Levi. It was important for Moses to control his anger. We are to approach people in God's wisdom and love so they will receive BENEFIT of confrontation (which is an alternative to unacceptable behavior).

    ■ Pray for God's wisdom; and,

    ■ Follow up with appropriate confrontation.

Let people know, if it is possible, that you are confronting them because you love them and want the best for them.

As parents, God tells us to correct without anger. We may have to spank (use the rod, not the hand) at times, but we should always, after the discipline, **pray with**

our children and let them KNOW they are FORGIVEN and LOVED. God did NOT invent "time out." "Time out" has probably done more to make it hard for young people to honor, hear from, and serve God than any other socially devised concept during the ages. It is probably one of the major factors for the increased number of teen pregnancies.

"And you, fathers, do not provoke your children to wrath, but bring them up in the training and admonition of the LORD." (Ephesians 6:4)

LET GOD FIGHT FOR YOU

After you have first prayed and done what God has showed you to do . . . then REST! We see two good examples of this in Exodus Chapter 14 and 2 Chronicles Chapter 20.

"Stand still, and see the salvation of the LORD, which He will accomplish for you today . . . the LORD will fight for you, and you shall hold your peace." (Exodus 13-14)
"Do not be afraid nor dismayed because of this great multitude, for the battle is not yours, but God's." (2 Chronicles 20:15)

We also see what happened to those who rebelled against Moses and Aaron in Numbers 16:28-30.

Has God ever lost a battle? NO! Have you? YES!

SEPARATE YOURSELF FROM STRIFE

When you need deliverance, separate yourself from struggle . . . and let God do a MIRACLE!

MENTALLY SEPARATE YOURSELF

If you are thinking negative thoughts, separate yourself from these and renew your mind with the promises in God's Word.

PHYSICALLY SEPARATE YOURSELF

You may have to separate yourself from either a SITUATION or a PERSON. In Exodus Chapter Two we read where Moses killed a man. He then spent 40 years in the wilderness of Midian, probably in the eastern part of the Sinai peninsula or northwestern Arabia. I, personally, have walked alone with 19 camels in that Sinai desert. There, under the tutelage of God, Moses learned how to control himself . . . and how to control a flock. After that, he became Israel's pastor for 40 years.

Think about YOUR lifestyle. **You may have to separate yourself from ungodly relationships** or counter-productive relationships.

INTERCEDE FOR OTHERS

Six times Moses interceded for the lives of Israel. On one occasion, God told Moses that he would even wipe out the complaining Israelites and give Moses a NEW nation, greater and mightier than they, to start over. However, Moses interceded for the people and talked God into sparing them. (Numbers 14:11-24)

After the incident where God judged Korah, Dathan, and Abiram, the children of Israel went immediately back to complaining, and accused Moses of killing them. Because of this, another 14,700 people died. (Numbers 16:41)

Notice, "the children of Korah died not." (Numbers 26:11) Years later, we read about the children (descendants) of Korah being ministers in the tabernacle (1 Chronicles 9:19). They also wrote many Psalms. God had warned the people to depart from the rebels and get away from their tents before judgment fell. Evidently, someone in Korah's family made a quality decision.

There is a truth here: **You may have to walk away from a relationship . . . or a relative . . . at some time in your life**. But only do it after MUCH PRAYER, seeking God's will and not yours; and KNOWING it is what God wants at that time! It doesn't mean that you don't love them, or that you're not willing to help them. Read Genesis Chapter 13 and Mark 10:29.

Above all, never forget what Jesus promised you, *"I will never leave you nor forsake you."* (Hebrews 13:5) And **... always forgive! Forgiveness can save most relationships**. God is our perfect model. In the *Book of Hosea*, God pictures Israel as a harlot gone away from her husband. After all the times Israel disobeyed God, as a disobedient wife, He still promises her a glorious future:

"I will betroth you to Me forever; yes I will betroth you to Me in righteousness and justice, in loving kindness and mercy; I will betroth you to me in faithfulness, and you shall know the LORD." (Hosea 2:19)

Now that you know the different personality dynamics involved—the different mentalities—and the processes for strengthening your inner being while dealing with tension, you are ready to learn categories of problems—classification of offenses—and **HOW to address them specifically: the Bible way!**

Your mental and emotional (and sometimes physical) well being—and, especially, your spiritual growth with the LORD—will depend upon your proactive stance in these matters. Don't worry ... if you have fear about confrontation ... the answer has been provided.

- Pray for God's wisdom; and,

- Follow up with appropriate confrontation.

Do what God tells you—then rest. He will take care of the other party or parties. Examples are following.

HOW TO RESOLVE CONFLICTS
THE BIBLE WAY

"We all stumble in many ways. If anyone is never at fault in what he says, he is a perfect man, able to keep his whole body in check." [James 3:2]

"Brethren, if someone is caught in a sin, you who are spiritual should restore him gently. But watch yourself, or you also may be tempted." [Galatians 6:2]

"Woe to the world because of the things that cause people to sin! Such things must come, but woe to the man through whom they come." [Matthew 18:7]

There are several categories of problems that must be addressed if we are to progress in our Christian walk. They are trespasses, offenses, or sins of the following nature:

    ■ If your brother trespasses against you ... [Matthew 18:15]

    ■ If you offend your brother. [Matthew 5:23-26]

    ■ Offenses against children [Matthew 18:1-6; 18:10,14]

- Offenses against the church; and

- Offenses against those outside the church. [I Corinthians 10:32]

IF YOUR BROTHER TRESPASSES AGAINST YOU

You are to forgive him! *"For if you forgive men their trespasses (offenses or misdeeds), your heavenly Father will also forgive you: but if you do not forgive men (for) their trespasses, neither will your Father forgive your trespasses."* [Matthew 6:14-15]

Go tell him, or show him, his fault or trespass, **just between the two of you**. If he listens to you, you have won your brother over; but if he will not listen, take one or two others along, so that 'every matter may be established by the testimony of two or three witnesses', as required by the law of Moses in Deuteronomy 19:15-17. [Matthew 18:15-16]

If he refuses to listen to them (the other witnesses), tell it to the church; and if he refuses to listen even to the church, treat him as you would a heathen (a non-Jew, or worshipper of a false God) or a tax collector. [Matthew 18:17]

IF YOU OFFEND YOUR BROTHER

If you remember that your (Christian) brother has something against you, go and be reconciled to your brother ...***

Settle matters **quickly** with an enemy who is taking you to court. Do it while you are still with him on the way (to court), or he may hand you over to the judge, and the judge may hand you over to the officer, and you may be thrown into prison—you will not get out until you have paid all your enemy can get. [Matthew 5:23-26]

***NOTE: If you are offering a special "seed offering" or gift to God, leave your gift; first go and be reconciled to your brother; then come and offer your gift.

OFFENSES AGAINST CHILDREN

Jesus placed **special importance** on the treatment of little children **especially children who believe on Him**. He said that whoever offends*** (or causes to stumble spiritually) a little child, will suffer great punishment. Always encourage little children to follow and love Jesus; help them in whatever way you can ... and remember, when you receive a little child in Jesus' name ... you receive Jesus! [Matthew 18:1-6]

Teach your people not to despise, nor to think badly, against a little child, for Jesus said, *"In heaven their angels do always behold the face of my Father which is in Heaven."* [Matthew 18:10]

*****NOTE:** Offended (def) = hurt; wounded; affronted; vexed.

OFFENSES AGAINST THE SYNAGOGUE OR THE CHURCH; AND THOSE OUTSIDE

As the church looks out to evangelize the world it sees lost Jews and lost Gentiles (non-Jews). The church or Messianic synagogue itself is made up of saved Jews and saved Gentiles (non-Jews). This is why 1 Corinthians 10:32 says, *"Give none offence, neither to the Jews, nor to the Gentiles, nor to the church of God."* [1 Corinthians 10:32] Notice the three (3) groups:

- Jews;

- Non-Jews (Gentiles); and,

- The church or the Messianic synagogue

Compare this with Ephesians 2:11-18.

Offenses against the church or synagogue may be categorized as follows:

■ Wounding the conscience of a brother—a fellow believer in Jesus, the Messiah;

■ Talking badly about, hurting, or opposing God's leaders;

■ Hindering (opposing, causing harm to, or slowing) the work of God;

■ Teaching false doctrine.

WOUNDING THE CONSCIENCE OF A CHRISTIAN BROTHER

There are some things that you know that **you** can do, that another Christian may not be able to do, because of conscience sake. For example, one Christian may feel in good conscience that he may drink wine, while another Christian may not. If the brother who does not feel he should drink wine (that is, he violates his own conscience by partaking) sees you drinking wine, he will be offended. You may cause him to stumble!

In such a case. the brother who feels he may partake should abstain at that present time, out of consideration for the other person and for the other person's conscience. Do not seek your own good and advantage and profit **...** but rather **seek the welfare of your brother** [1 Corinthians 10:24]. All things are permissible, but **not all things are helpful or profitable or wholesome**. All things are legitimate, but **not all things are constructive to character** and building spiritual life [Verse 23].

Make up your mind not to put any stumbling block or obstacle in your brother's way. If your brother is distressed because of what you eat, you are no longer acting in love. **Do not by your actions destroy your brother for whom Christ died**. It is better not to drink wine or to do anything else that will cause your brother to fall.

The Scripture says, *"Do you have faith? Whatever you believe about these things, keep between yourself and God. Blessed is the man who does not condemn himself by what he approves. But the man who has doubts is condemned if he does NOT act from faith. Everything that does not come from faith is sin ... whatever is done without a conviction of its approval by God is sinful."* [Romans 14:22-23]

TALKING BADLY ABOUT, HURTING OR OPPOSING GOD'S LEADERS

Many Christians, as well as other people, are sick, poor, or have died because of their actions, thoughts, or attitudes against a servant of God.

The Scriptures abound with true-life examples of the above and the resultant judgments. In 1 Samuel Chapters 24 and 26 we read interesting accounts that describe the character of (King) David. King Saul had been hunting him to kill him, with 3,000 chosen men out of Israel.

Twice David had an opportunity to kill Saul but each time he refused to do so. David said, *"Destroy him not: for who can stretch forth his hand against the Lord's anointed, and be guiltless? ... The Lord forbid that I should stretch forth mine hand against the Lord's anointed."*

Rebellion is as the sin of witchcraft, and since Saul rebelled against God's new choice of a leader in David (the "old order" versus the "new order") he ended up seeking help from the witch of Endor, who was a servant of the defeated one, Satan. [1 Samuel 28] **You**

are who you run with! If you don't want fleas, don't lie down with the dogs!

Guard your spirit! Saul had been anointed with oil to be King over Israel by Samuel the Prophet. Because of disobedience Saul was rejected as king by God two times [1 Samuel Chapters 13 and 15], and God then chose David [1 Samuel 16]. **Never think evil of or do evil or say evil to—or about—a minister of Messiah Jesus!** Do NOT allow jealousy, rebellion, hatred, or strife to be part of your life ... especially as relates to ministry!

Following are a few examples of what happened when people took part in actions, thoughts, or attitudes against God's leaders. Read through these examples carefully (there are many more in the Holy Bible); let God speak to you and then teach your people!

> ▪ Trying to deceive or lie to a man of God [2 Kings 5:15-27]

> ▪ Hurting them physically [1 Kings 13:1-6]

> ▪ Causing them anguish or mental stress [2 Kings 2:23-21]

■ Slandering them or gossiping about them [Genesis 37-45]

■ Hindering the work of God [Acts 13:6-12]

■ Thinking or wishing evil toward them [Esther 9:24-25]

■ Rebellion against God's leaders [Numbers 12:1-16]

■ Trying to make out with a minister's wife [Genesis 12:14-20, Genesis 20:1-18, and Genesis 26:6-11]

Notice that **whole nations** were in danger of judgment when men tried to have a relationship with an anointed man's wife ... **even though they didn't know** the woman was married!

About 50 years ago I took a preacher's wife to a drama. I had invited her and another Christian sister when he was out of town ministering. I was a fairly new Christian and a foolish young man. I made no approaches that would seem to myself, or to other people, improper. However, I sinned a great sin—in ignorance—against an anointed man of God.

26

You may always weigh every deed and thought by this commandment: *"Therefore all things whatsoever you would that men should do to you, you do even so to them: for this is the law and the prophets."* [Jesus - Matthew 7:12]

Several years ago a Christian lady who lived only one block (about 100 meters) from my family came to our home while I was gone and **gave a false prophecy against me to one of the family members. Within 24 hours her whole house was destroyed to the ground ... without one stick of wood remaining**. She was left with no place to live for her or her children.

You need to teach your people—and others—these truths. Their lives, their health, their prosperity, their minds and their spiritual well-being—and their families—may be in jeopardy if you don't! Don't be slow to tell people, **"Don't mess with me or my family ... I'm a man (or, woman) of God!"**

HINDERING THE WORK OF GOD

Even little things that hinder or slow down God's work are "weighty" in the eyes of God. People are generally ignorant concerning the anointing, the office of the anointing, and the anointed person.

Several years ago a delivery truck driver left a small inexpensive package for me at a neighbor's house. **It was to be used in God's work**. I didn't realize why I had not received it and one day the neighbor—who owned a liquor store—finally said they had the package. The neighbor was outside on the walk getting groceries out of her car and would not take the time to go into their house and get the package for us.

Shortly after, the neighbor drove her brand new Cadillac (one of the most expensive cars made in USA) into her garage—it would NOT stop—the car crashed through the back wall of the garage and **drove into the swimming pool in the back yard and sunk**.

The lady was blessed that she did not drown. She never got her car back and **she was the "laughing stock" of three major cities** as her story was on the front page of three very large newspapers. **Don't mess with God's work ... or His workers!**

One time, in a position of authority where God had placed me—it was a secular position, but one that enabled me to do God's work—**a man who was drunk was hindering me**. I spoke the Word of God to him, and as I had my back to him he—probably the demon in him—picked up a large glass ashtray to hit me.

God spoke to me instantly and emphatically, "Let me handle this!" If I had tried to struggle in the flesh, I would have been doing just what the enemy wanted. **The next day the man died of a brain hemorrhage**. He was a young man in his 30's. God did handle it for me. **Don't mess with God's work ... or His workers!**

Several years ago a preacher and pastor, who I had helped much spiritually and materially, deceived me in a matter of courtship with a young lady. I had asked him different times, "Is there anything I need to know about her?" "Does she really love Jesus and is she really dedicated to Christ?" She appeared outwardly one way, but in my spirit I felt doubtful. The pastor kept assuring me of her dedication.

His lack of honesty, perhaps for financial gain, caused much trouble to me personally and to the work of God. Shortly after that, he became ill, lost much weight, and **finally died** young—leaving behind a widow and three young children. Always be honest with a man of God. **Don't mess with God's work ... or His workers!**

People who are relatives of a man of God have to be very careful. But, on the other hand, they have tremendous opportunity to be blessed! Here's an example from the Holy Bible: After a great victory, King David returned to bless his household. His wife, Michal, spoke badly toward him because she had seen him dancing and praising the LORD openly among other maidens. Because of her attitude towards her husband and her words to him, **she had no child unto the day of her death**. [2 Samuel 6:20-23] She turned an opportunity to be blessed into a curse!

My in-laws had vexed me for years: in my personal life, in my marriage, and in my ministry. I had liked my father-in-law and had looked forward to him living with us someday after he retired and was old. One day I found out that he had said three (3) very ugly and untrue things about me. **He died a while later of a very cruel and extremely painful death**.

I had gone to the hospital at God's direction (a long distance away) to visit him. The Lord showed me he needed to be able to talk to me in person and ask for

30

forgiveness. When I arrived at the hospital, his wife, the mother-in-law, had instructed the hospital personnel not to allow me to visit him. He died there ... unable to clear himself with me personally.

The mother-in-law was demon-possessed. Several ministers had told her this through the years, men that I didn't even know. One time I took her to a very large Christian meeting held by a seasoned man of God who had ministered and raised up churches for around 50 years.

The man of God did not know her—or me—in a personal way. We were seated toward the back of a very large crowd, and **the preacher looked back and told her, "You have a demon!" ...** and then he named the demon! **Then he looked at me and said, "You are transitioning into your apostolic ministry!"**

She continued to cause much trouble with me, my family, and my ministry. Finally, I told her one day, **"Get your house in order.** You are going to die for putting your hand to God's work!" Not long after, she died a terrible death, also. Both of the in-laws named the name of Jesus. I have long since forgiven them, but they turned an opportunity to be blessed into a curse!

One of the churches where I was pastor years ago was really under a blessing of God; I had ordained the Senior Pastor before me and the Senior Pastor before him. God was doing wonderful miracles of healing and in the lives of people. Also, we were producing about 250,000 pieces of literature a week; not to mention radio programs and tapes.

I made a big mistake when I became Senior Pastor. Because I knew several of the families there and also had ordained one of my assistants (the former Senior Pastor), **I trusted everyone—I never made sure I had control of the church**. Unknown to me was demonic activity manifesting itself mainly in **jealousies**. As far as the ministry, my heart was pure; but overnight God's work was brought to a screaming halt.

A few people were mad because I had removed some people from their positions (some were their family members) and reduced the salary of others who I felt were receiving too much money. The church was then taken over by a rebellious faction. The city where this happened had never experienced a violent catastrophe, at least to my knowledge. Not long after,

that city became the epicenter for a devastating earthquake! And God directed me into better fields!!

There was a young minister who was a personal acquaintance of mine. I had ordained him into the ministry. He was a good husband and father of three children. He had wonderful compassion for people. I had some fruitful ministry in meetings he organized. Over a period of time he began to observe some abuses in a very well-known, and anointed, church where I taught as a professor in the graduate school of theology.

He began to be bitter and talk about some of the ministers including the Senior Pastor who was—and still is—a wonderful man of God. He should first have gone and talked to the people involved, as is outlined in this book under *"If Your Brother Trespasses Against You."*

Instead of praying for the people and letting God deal with the situation, **he became more bitter and slanderous**. One day as he was driving down the freeway a small piece of metal fell off the back of **a truck and went through his windshield, striking him**

in the middle of the forehead. He died as a result, leaving a widow and three very young children.

I have used several personal examples in this book. Some have been "buried" in my heart for years; but if they help you, or one of God's workers, to escape the deception and tricks of the enemy—and to become stronger in Christ—then I am glad to have shared them!

Honor the anointing, and the anointed person, as well as the anointed office (or, position of authority set by God). Always use King David as an example in this regard and you'll be safe!

As a young minister I attended Kathryn Kuhlman's meetings whenever I could. Among many things I learned was the following:

The Holy Spirit is God's agent on earth to supply the resurrection power of Christ!

Be careful how you treat Him ... and speak about him! **Honor the Holy Spirit ... and He will honor you!**

TEACHING FALSE DOCTRINE

This offense is **BOTH** against those inside the Church or Messianic synagogue and against those outside. You must protect your sheep—and other sheep. We are to bear one another's burdens [Galatians 6:2]. In some respect, just as in evangelism, we must also inform those outside the house of faith of false doctrine. However, don't let the devil run you ragged! You could chase around trying to correct false doctrines all of your life!

The cults have all have at least one of **three errors** (if not all three). They teach:

▪ Jesus was NOT God in human flesh;

▪ You can work your way to Heaven;

▪ Hell is not real (or, if it is, it only lasts for a short period).

Be led by the Spirit of God! Follow the plain teachings of Jesus. **Preach and teach the simple Gospel, apart from which there is no other gospel** [1 Corinthians 15:1-5]. Obey the commission of Jesus in Matthew 28 and Mark 16. Adhere to the "Apostles' Creed". Use the pastoral writings of Paul and Peter and John as examples for church order and discipline, and obey the Word of God as revealed in the Holy Bible.

A three-fold cord is not easily broken. Buildings designed in triangulation or with three-sided segments are stronger. Jesus sent out his apostles to:

- Preach and teach;

- Heal; and,

- Cast out demons.

Whether you are involved in ministry to governments, to the homeless, to the military—in person, in the media or on the internet—keep your ministry "triangulated" **in balance** with Jesus' authority that he gave you: to preach; to heal; and, to cast out demons!

Then you won't have to worry about false doctrines ... because **no one can copy the works God is doing through you**. The Lord will confirm the Word of God you preach with signs following ... and people who are really seeking God will come to the TRUTH!

No false teaching in the world can do **all three** ... present the Good News, heal, and cast out demons!

36

Especially like you are doing when you're anointed with LOVE! False teaching is usually "lop-sided" with emphasis on either of **two large errors**: **1.** Either you're saved by your works only; or, **2.** You can sin all you want to and get away with it.

"Faith without works is dead." [James 2:14-26]

"For in Messiah Jesus neither circumcision avails anything, nor uncircumcision; but faith which works by love." [Galatians 5:6]

FINAL THOUGHTS

When you have done everything you know to do—or, that you have been instructed by the LORD to do—concerning bringing resolution and healing to a relationship, **then rest. Leave it in the LORD's hands**. Do not feel condemned. God knows how to deal with the other party(s) … and He knows you have done your part. Continue to pray for the healing power of Jesus to invade the situation. **Release the situation to Him**.

I trust this book will help you to resolve ALL of your conflicts—especially to do what YOU need to do—and to have an extremely fruitful, blessed and peaceful life during your remaining years on Planet Earth!

Here's a promise for YOU. I have seen many MIRACLES claiming this promise from GOD:

"Call to me and I will answer you, and show you great and mighty things which you do not know."
– Tanakh: Jeremiah 33:3

LIVE A LIFE OF EXCELLENCE!

See following pages for Bonus & Announcement

OTHER BOOKS BY PRINCE HANDLEY

- Map of the End Times
- How to Do Great Works
- Flow Chart of Revelation
- Action Keys for Success
- Health and Healing Complete Guide to Wholeness
- Prophetic Calendar for Israel & the Nations: Thru 2023
- Healing Deliverance
- How to Receive God's Power with Gifts of the Spirit
- Healing for Mental and Physical Abuse
- Victory Over Opposition and Resistance
- Healing of Emotional Wounds
- How to Be Healed and Live in Divine Health
- Healing from Fear, Shame and Anger
- How to Receive Healing and Bring Healing to Others
- New Global Strategy: Enabling Missions
- The Art of Christian Warfare
- Success Cycles and Secrets
- New Testament Bible Studies (A Study Manual)
- Babylon the Bitch – Enemy of Israel
- Resurrection Multiplication – Miracle Production
- Faith and Quantum Physics – Your Future

AVAILABLE AT AMAZON AND OTHER BOOK STORES

For updates go here > www.marketplaceworld.com

UNIVERSITY OF EXCELLENCE PRESS

Los Angeles ◼ London ◼ Tel Aviv

BONUS

To help you, and to help you teach others, we have prepared Rabbinical Studies at this site:

http://www.uofe.org/RABBINICAL_STUDIES.html

These are commentaries from **ancient** Jewish Rabbis that identify the Mashiach of Israel.

To help you, and to help you teach others, we have also prepared Bible Studies in English, Spanish and French.

- English FREE Bible Studies
  http://www.uofe.org/english_bible_studies.html
- Spanish FREE Bible Studies
  http://www.uofe.org/spanish_bible_studies.html
- French FREE Bible Studies
  http://www.uofe.org/french_bible_studies.html

ANNOUNCEMENT

We recommend the companion books to this book.

Healing of Emotional Wounds

Healing for Mental and Physical Abuse

Victory Over Opposition and Resistance

Health and Healing Complete Guide to Wholeness

All available at Amazon and other book stores.

✚

NOTE

For seminars with Prince Handley, contact:
princehandley@gmail.com.

UNIVERSITY OF EXCELLENCE PRESS
Los Angeles ■ London ■ Tel Aviv

NOTE

We listen to our readers. Tell us what **new** subject
matter you would like to see published. Email your
ideas to: universityofexcellence@gmail.com.

www.ingramcontent.com/pod-product-compliance
Lightning Source LLC
Chambersburg PA
CBHW060634030426
42337CB00018B/3349